AN ADVENT EXPERIENCE

Paul Sheneman

illumina

BEACON HILL PRESS
OF KANSAS CITY

Copyright 2011 by Beacon Hill Press of Kansas City
ISBN 978-0-8341-2772-2

Printed in the
United States of America

Cover: Lindsey McCormack
Interior Design: Lindsey McCormack

Unless otherwise indicated, all Scripture quotations are taken from the *Holy Bible, New International Version*® (NIV®). Copyright © 1973, 1978, 1984 by Biblica, Inc.™ Used by permission of Zondervan. All rights reserved worldwide. www.zondervan.com.

Scripture quotations marked KJV are from the King James Version.

Permission to quote from the following additional copyrighted versions of the Bible is acknowledged with appreciation:

The Holy Bible, English Standard Version® (ESV®), copyright © 2001 by Crossway, a publishing ministry of Good News Publishers. All rights reserved.

The *New Revised Standard Version* (NRSV) of the Bible, copyright 1989 by the Division of Christian Education of the National Council of the Churches of Christ in the USA. Used by permission. All rights reserved.

The *Revised Standard Version* (RSV) of the Bible, copyright 1946, 1952, 1971 by the Division of Christian Education of the National Council of the Churches of Christ in the USA.

Acknowledgment is gratefully given to Merritt J. Nielson for contributing the Advent Sunday devotional reflections.

10 9 8 7 6 5 4 3 2 1

The light shines
in the darkness,
and the darkness has
not overcome it.

—John 1:5, ESV

contents

INTRODUCTION

Advent announces the arrival of a new year for Christians. It is the first season on the Christian calendar. During Advent we remember and celebrate important events and get ready for others.

Beginning four weeks before Christmas, the season of Advent is supposed to be a special time of waiting and preparing. It is a time when Christians get ready to experience again the story of God's Messiah, Jesus—the Light of the World—who came to the people of Israel over two thousand years ago to rescue a world darkened by suffering, death, and pain. Advent is also a time when Christians embrace the hope that Jesus will come again.

During this time of year we celebrate the good news that the Light of Jesus has pierced the darkness of evil. At first the Light was only a dim glow, a point of light envisioned by prophets. But then it sparkled to life as a baby in a manger. From this small beginning, the Light has grown and spread, overtaking the darkness, so that someday the darkness will be no more. The world will wake up to the dawn of a new day. It will be reborn as a new creation. During Advent we celebrate the coming of this Light and look forward to it illuminating the entire world.

But Advent is more than just waiting for the darkness to end. It is also about helping to overcome that darkness. As children of the Light, we share in the Light and bear the Light everywhere we go. We are to shine as rays of hope to all we meet by what we do, what we say, and how we live. As we travel the road to Advent, we are to illuminate the world around us.

So let's join together and begin our Advent journey. As we embrace the familiar practices of prayer, storytelling, Scripture reading, holy conversation, and acts of mercy, we hope to bask in the hope, love, joy, and peace of the Light and then share the Light, and all its gifts, with others. In this ordinary path of watching, waiting, living, and doing, we will experience the extraordinary—that God came to us once as a helpless infant and he will come again as our reigning Savior and Lord.

FAMILY

This is a guide for families to journey into the experience of Advent.

But this guide isn't *just* for families the way we usually think of families. You know, moms, dads, grandpas, grandmas, guardians, aunts, uncles, brothers, and sisters.

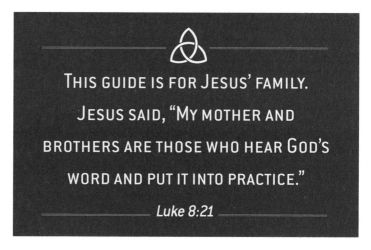

THIS GUIDE IS FOR JESUS' FAMILY. JESUS SAID, "MY MOTHER AND BROTHERS ARE THOSE WHO HEAR GOD'S WORD AND PUT IT INTO PRACTICE."

Luke 8:21

You see, God adopted us in Jesus. He calls us all children of the light. And Jesus told us to love one another (John 15). We need to keep this in mind on our Advent journey. We are traveling it as members of Jesus' family. God has made us one of his own.

But what about our own families—the people we live with and are related to?

This guide is designed to help local churches disciple these families through the Advent season. An important emphasis in this guide is that each household is called to be a little church or missionary outpost. In other words, every family is to become an expression of the family of God.

But not everyone lives in a family. Some Christians live by themselves. How are they going to use this guide? They have a

family in their brothers and sisters in Christ. See how being a member of Jesus' family works? We are all responsible for making sure no one goes through this Advent journey alone. That might mean including in our own household a brother or sister in Christ. Or it might mean single Christians gathering together as a family in Christ. Everyone is a member of a family and can travel the road of Advent in the company of others.

FAMILY DEVOTIONAL GUIDE

Every local church is different. Yours may have some practices and traditions for observing Advent and Christmas that others don't have. But there are some traditions many churches have in common. This resource focuses on two practices that are part of this common tradition: the lighting of the Advent wreath and the use of the *Revised Common Lectionary*. Both are adapted for use by families as they journey through Advent.

SUNDAY DEVOTIONS

The Sunday devotional reflections are designed to get your family ready for small-group study and worship. These reflections will introduce the gospel reading and main theme of the passage. The "Prepare for Worship" section introduces each week's candle and what it represents.

WEEKDAY AND SATURDAY DEVOTIONS

The weekday devotions are divided into sections: First, the section called Connection is a daily way to connect the Advent wreath to family life. Through this section your family will explore the weekly theme of the Advent wreath. As they progress through this section, family members will find opportunities to engage in conversations, develop family traditions, and experience growth in God's grace.

The second section consists of family devotions. These gospel readings follow the readings for Year Two of the "Daily Office Lectionary" in the *Book of Common Prayer*. These readings will connect your family to the Scripture readings that millions of Christian brothers and sisters are following. As your family members walk through these familiar stories with the family of God, they will experience the possibility of having a deeper and more faithful relationship with God.

AN ADVENT EXPERIENCE

This resource is only a guide. Lives get busy during this time of the year, and making life busier is not the goal of this resource. The devotionals, readings, and other materials are all designed to help you enter more deeply into specific faith practices so that you can grow in God's grace. So we are giving you permission upfront to use this resource in a way that fits your lifestyle. If you have time to do all the daily devotions and readings, that's great. But if not, that's okay too. We want you to use this as a means of God's grace for your family in a way that works best for your family. We want you and your family to be free to enter fully into the Advent experience.

ADVENT SEASON • WEEK ONE

THE RETURN OF MISS KENYON
A Devotional Reflection Based on Mark 13:24-37

The intercom at Fairlawn School crackled out: "Miss Kenyon, could you come to my office?" It was Miss Morris, the principal. Miss Kenyon, our pleasant but strict sixth grade teacher, turned to us and said, "Read the next chapter in your literature book. You'll be having a test when I return." We all answered, "Yes, Miss Kenyon."

As her high-heeled shoes clicked down the stairs, we all sat quietly for a few minutes, half-heartedly leafing through our literature books. Several more minutes passed, and Miss Kenyon still hadn't returned. Suddenly a spitball flew across the room, followed by some paper airplanes, and then more spitballs. One classmate challenged another, and a fight broke out. Someone yelled at Patsy Thelig and she ran past my desk, knocking me in the face with her elbow and sending my glasses flying onto the radiator. A lens shattered. Then there was a scramble of feet and everything got very quiet. Looking up through my cracked lens, I spied Miss Kenyon standing at the door, hands on her hips, and an angry look on her face. None of us were prepared for what followed—a test that none of us could pass and a one-hour after-school detention every day for a week!

What happened in Miss Kenyon's classroom is very similar to what Jesus is talking about in our gospel passage. Jesus, warning his disciples about end-time calamities and his sudden return, urged them to "beware . . . for you do not know when the time will come" (v. 33, NRSV). Then Jesus tells a story: "James, John, Peter, Andrew, it's like this. A man goes on a journey and leaves the servants in charge of his sprawling estate. He tells the doorman to be especially watchful, because the owner could return unexpectedly and he doesn't want to find his servants unprepared" (see v. 34).

Through this parable Jesus was continuing his response to a question from the disciples after he had predicted the destruction of the Jewish temple in Jerusalem (see vv. 1-4). The disciples had asked, "Tell us, when will this be, and what will be the sign that all these things are about to be accomplished?" (v. 4, NRSV). Jesus began his response by speaking about the coming of wars, earthquakes, famines, persecutions, betrayals, and sufferings unknown from the beginning of creation (see vv. 5-13). His urgent word about all these things to them, as well as to us, was, "Therefore, keep awake . . . or else he may find you asleep when he comes suddenly" (vv. 35-36, NRSV).

The message of Advent on this first Sunday is straightforward: Jesus is coming again, and unexpectedly. Miss Kenyon never told us *when* she would be back. She just showed up when her business with Miss Morris was done, and we were unprepared. When Jesus comes again, there won't be any time to get ready. We will need to *be* ready, or we will flunk life's most important test. "Beware, keep alert; for you do not know when the time will come" (v. 33, NRSV).

We discover that the first concerns of the church calendar for the beginning of a new Christian year are not chronological ones. Instead, the church's doorway to yet another year of illuminating the gospel story—remembering, rehearsing, and retelling God's redemptive purposes for humankind—is the bold proclamation of Christ's *coming again*. Accompanying this proclamation is a deep longing for God to speak, intervene, and come close to us in power and glory. It's a little tricky, like patting your head and rubbing your stomach at the same time, but the gospel calls us to keep one eye on the future, asking God to hasten the day of Christ's appearing, while we keep another eye on the present, doing the things that the faithful servant is expected to do while the master of the house is away.

So our journey to Bethlehem begins with a vision of the way God will bring the world's story to an end. The final events are filled with turmoil and confusion among nations and people. Even the world of nature reels in distress. The scriptures that call us to the mysteries of Christmas urge us first to prepare for the end of time, for the appearance of Christ, the Son of God, the Judge before whom we all must stand. They warn us to be ready. They invite us to examine our hearts and commitments, to make sure that cares, anxieties, and enslaving habits and practices aren't weighing us down and draining our energies, while they also keep us from entering too quickly into the Christmas story.

During Advent, we are not counting down the days to Christmas, nor are we jumping immediately into Bethlehem's magnificent story. No, we are listening intently to Christ's provocative words about the end of all things, about God's plan to vindicate his purposes and establish his kingdom completely and forever. At any moment Jesus could be standing at the door, and we don't want to be caught unprepared. That doesn't mean we should live in fear of the apocalyptic calamities described in today's scripture. Instead, we should embrace the words of hope illuminating the pathway to Bethlehem's manger: "Heaven and earth will pass away, but my words will not pass away" (v. 31, NRSV). Thanks be to God!

PREPARE FOR WORSHIP—THE PROPHETS' CANDLE
First Sunday of Advent

The first candle of Advent is the prophets' candle, which symbolizes hope. As the prophets of Israel received from God messages of hope about his promise to heal and reclaim Israel, we also receive that message today. The flicker of a single flame reminds us that the Light of World, Jesus, has already come. However, Jesus has not yet returned to complete the work he started. We wait and anticipate the second coming of the Son of God in order that the world may be rid of all darkness. Today, we are called to recognize the darkness and to hope in the Light.

MONDAY •

=== **DAILY PSALM** ===

*I will give thanks to the L*ORD *because of his righteousness and will sing praise to the name of the L*ORD *Most High.*

—————— **PSALM 7:17** ——————

 ## CONNECTION

HOPE

Our Advent journey begins in almost complete darkness. But we see the faint hope of a flickering light that has started pushing back the darkness. The sight should inspire us to hope in the Light, Jesus, who has come and will come again.

Hope is an odd thing to understand. We typically think of hope as a good thing. Yet hope is rarely found in places where good things happen regularly. Rather, hope is found in places where bad things happen, such as when we experience hurt and loss. So if you meet people who are hopeful, they can usually tell you stories of pain or suffering.

Christian hope embraces two truths. The first truth is that we live in a world of pain and suffering. Embracing the truth of a suffering world affects the way we view the world and interact with others. The second truth is that there is a good God who can and will heal the pain and suffering in the world. In Advent we retell the story of this good and powerful God who came in the form of a little baby to heal the hurting world.

During worship we lit the prophets' candle, which symbolizes hope. Now we are sent to watch for and live as signs of hope in the world. The aim for us this week is to search for the light of hope in others, in ourselves, and in the world.

FAMILY DEVOTIONS
Light the Advent candle • Gospel Reading: Matt. 21:1-11

HOPE IN THE GENTLE KING

We are entering a difficult time of the year. Planning and shopping for parties, church activities, family get-togethers, and travel create a stressful environment of exhausted people. Competitive shoppers push and force their way through crowds to get the latest and greatest Christmas gift. And TV commercials promote the latest video games and electronic gadgets as ideal presents for those on any gift list. All of it leaves you wondering if the season's spirit of joy and generosity has been replaced with stress, struggle, and competition.

We turn to Jesus' story and see him also entering a difficult situation. We are told that Jesus enters Jerusalem in fulfillment of an Old Testament prophecy about God's chosen one. The action shakes the city and creates a dangerous environment for Jesus. The religious leaders, fearing Jesus and his teaching, will eventually plot to kill him.

Yet Jesus doesn't choose to enter the city with force, and he doesn't choose to slip in unnoticed either. Jesus chooses to enter Jerusalem and face the dangers awaiting him without being violent. He teaches us not to fight evil but to turn the other cheek in love (5:39-40). So we are asked by the gentle King to follow him into this season with the hope that we can witness to his light. Instead of succumbing to the tension and struggle that so often mars this time of year, we can be bearers of peace and love, a soothing presence through whom others can see Jesus shining.

=== **PRAYER** ===

Hosanna to the living Lord! Hosanna to the Incarnate Word! To Christ, Creator, Savior, King, let earth, let heaven, Hosanna ring![1]

—— AMEN ——

=== **DAILY PSALM** ===

Give ear to my words, O Lord, consider my sighing. Listen to my cry for help, my King and my God, for to you I pray. In the morning, O Lord, you hear my voice; in the morning I lay my requests before you and wait in expectation.

—— **PSALM 5:1–3** ——

 ## CONNECTION

HOPE PROJECTS

Are you ready to practice being the light of hope?

Below are some ideas to help fuel your imagination. Talk them over with your friends and family and decide on something all of you want to do. Try to pick one that you won't just do this year but that you will do each year as a tradition.

EXTEND YOUR FAMILY
Invite a friend or acquaintance who can't get home to his or her family into your family for Advent and Christmas.

LATE NIGHT CRAM
Final exams are in full swing. Create a cram session survival kit with snacks, school supplies, gift cards, encouraging notes, and other items, and mail or deliver it to a college student.

DON'T CELEBRATE CHRISTMAS . . . YET
Wait to put up all your Christmas decorations and lights. Put it off until the third week of Advent, when the theme is joy, or get extreme and have a family hanging of the greens on Christmas Eve. The goal is not to encourage procrastination but to experience Advent as the unique and separate season it is.

SHOVEL PATROL
Go out and shovel the snow from your neighbor's drive.

FAMILY ADVENT WREATH

As a family, plan, shop for materials, and make an Advent wreath together.

 FAMILY DEVOTIONS
Light the Advent candle • Gospel Reading: Matt. 21:12-22

HOPE AND PRAY

Being with friends and family can be a mixed blessing. Family gatherings during this time of the year can be energizing and fun, even if family members don't always get along well. But sometimes there are broken relationships and rifts in a family that are a source of pain. When we are experiencing this kind of hurt, how do we deal with it?

Jesus' story teaches us that God can transform painful relationships. In both the temple scene and the story about the wilting of the fig tree, Jesus teaches the importance of prayer in the midst of our brokenness. He explains that if we pray while trusting God, the impossible can happen. God has the power to move mountains, heal the sick, give sight to the blind, and care for our hurting relationships.

We are invited to hope in God and continue to pray with complete trust that God will transform us and our relationships. You can trust in God's love and power as you prepare for times with friends and family. He will lead you in paths of peace as you trust in him.

The Light of the World is coming, and when he appears, he will heal our deepest hurts.

=== **PRAYER** ===

O very God of very God, and very Light of very Light, whose feet this earth's dark valley walked so it might be bright, we wait in faith and turn our face to where the daylight springs, until you will come, our gloom to chase, with healing in your wings.[2]

— **AMEN** —

=== **DAILY PSALM** ===

Look on me and answer, O LORD my God. Give light to my eyes, or I will sleep in death.

———————————— PSALM 13:3 ————————————

CONNECTION

THE SYMBOLISM OF THE ADVENT WREATH

The circle of the Advent wreath is an endless loop and reminds us of the eternal and endless love of God. Remember back to the very beginning of our story with God. In the beginning, God created all things in heaven and on earth. God created man and woman in his image. God gave man and woman the task to care for the world.

They lived in the goodness of God's creation with only one rule. They were told not to eat from one tree. They decided to break God's rule, and that is when sin and death entered the world.

Now we wait and hope in God, whose love is endless. Sin and death are a part of our world, but we also know that God's endless love has and will defeat them. So we wait in hope for the Light of God to come.

HOPE IN THE INVITATION

During Advent, Christians do unusual things. We sing songs to our neighbors. We make food for strangers. We give large sums of money to unknown people. And we spend time lighting candles and reading a Book. The curious observer might ask, "What does all this mean?"

Jesus is confronted by religious leaders and questioned about some unusual things he recently did. They ask Jesus where his authority comes from. The religious leaders want to know if what Jesus is doing is meaningful to them. For them it all depends on whether or not Jesus' authority is from God. But instead of answering, Jesus lays the responsibility to answer on them. Jesus invites them to either believe or reject him and God's authority.

We are called to follow Jesus' example this Advent season. To the curious observer we are called to bear witness that we are representatives of God and that we are preparing for the Light of the World. Just as Jesus gave the invitation to all people— including the outcasts in society, like the tax collector and prostitute—we are called to give everyone the opportunity to respond if what we do is meaningful to them.

=== **PRAYER** ===

The King shall come when morning dawns and light and beauty bring. Hail, Christ the Lord! Your people pray, come quickly, King of kings.[3]

AMEN

THURSDAY •

DAILY PSALM

I love you, O LORD, my strength. The LORD is my rock, my fortress and my deliverer; my God is my rock, in whom I take refuge. He is my shield and the horn of my salvation, my stronghold.

——— PSALM 18:1–2 ———

 CONNECTION

FAMILY STORIES OF HOPE

Today, connect your family stories to this week's Advent theme of hope. Think about how you can begin sharing your family stories of hope in God.

ENGAGE

Idea 1: Give everyone in the family a piece of paper. Ask each person to write down five things or draw a picture of something he or she hopes will happen. Give everyone a chance to share his or her hopes.

Idea 2: Ask everyone in the family to find one possession that helps him or her feel hopeful. Invite each one to share it and to tell why the object is a reminder of hope.

DISCUSS
• What does hope feel like?
• What is a hope you had that has been fulfilled?
• How has hope in God helped you in hard times?

HOPE IN THE RESPONSIBILITY

During the Advent season, friends and family sometimes assign us responsibilities we really don't want to do. Putting up lights, planning the family get-together, directing the children's play, and cooking food for parties are just some of the responsibilities that come up at this time. And these are all good, but if we do not want to do them, they could lead us to regret or even dread preparing for the celebration of Christ's birth. Sometimes we just lose sight of our priorities during this time of year.

In our gospel story, Jesus involves us in a huge responsibility. In the story, Jesus is rejecting the Jewish leadership—"the chief priests and the Pharisees"—and they know it (v. 45). Jesus says that the responsibilities of the kingdom of God will be given to others (v. 43). And we are those others if we believe in Jesus as our Savior and faithfully follow him. We are invited to be the light of God to the world.

The responsibility of being faithful followers of Jesus is the responsibility that should set our priorities for Advent. As you seek first the kingdom of God, all those other responsibilities will fall into place.

=== **PRAYER** ===

O Son of God, we wait for you in love for your appearing. We know you sit on the throne, and we, your name, are bearing.[4]

— AMEN —

FRIDAY • HOPE IN THE LIGHT

Therefore my heart is glad and my tongue rejoices; my body also will rest secure, because you will not abandon me to the grave, nor will you let your Holy One see decay. You have made known to me the path of life; you will fill me with joy in your presence, with eternal pleasures at your right hand

──────────── **PSALM 16:9–11** ────────────

 CONNECTION

SYMBOLS OF THE SEASON—CANDLE

The candle has long been a symbol of Christ, the Light of the World, even before the observance of Advent. The practice of using a candle to symbolize Christ probably came from the use of light as a metaphor for Jesus in the New Testament. The candle is also a great reminder to us during Advent that a part of our preparation is to spread the light of hope to our world.

HOPE IN A WARNING

The preparation for Christmas during the season of Advent is similar to the story Jesus tells in the gospel reading. We are invited to the celebration of a king. There are those who are asked to come but who do not accept the invitation. There are those who are invited and joyously accept the offer and faithfully prepare to attend. All are warned about how to prepare. We are to prepare by watching and hoping for the coming celebration of the king. Yet there are some who will come but who will not prepare properly.

What will happen?

If our life is like the story, then we will be rejected by the king. That is, we will not experience the joy and celebration of Christmas. We'll miss the purpose of the season and so much more.

But there is hope in the warning. We still have all of Advent to prepare by praying, sharing the light of God with others, seeking opportunities to be with God, and anticipating the coming Light by sharing stories of hope with friends and family. We still have time to prepare for the celebration of our king. So let's enter into the story.

===== **PRAYER** =====

O Christ, our true and only Light, illumine those who sit in night.[5]

———— **AMEN** ————

SATURDAY • HOPE IN THE LIGHT

━━━━━━━━━ **DAILY PSALM** ━━━━━━━━━

*Be exalted, O L*ORD*, in your strength; we will sing and praise your might.*

━━━━━━━ PSALM 21:13 ━━━━━━━

 CONNECTION

REFLECTION ON THE WEEK TOGETHER

- Where did you see God at work in your week?

- What did you learn about hope this week?

- How did you practice being a light of hope?

HOPE IN THE GIVER OF LIFE

We give ourselves to several things during the season of Advent. We deck the halls with family and friends. We make extra trips to the store or spend more time online searching for gifts. We rearrange our schedules to make an appearance at the work party. These activities are neither good nor bad—they are just typical of the season.

In our reading today, Jesus is questioned about a typical activity of his day. Religious leaders ask him about paying taxes to Caesar. They are hoping his answer will cause him to lose some credibility with his followers. They think that if Jesus affirms the payment of taxes, he would be affirming the Roman occupation, and this would offend his followers. But if Jesus denies the Roman right to tax the people, the religious leaders could report him to the local Roman authorities.

Yet Jesus neither affirms Roman occupation nor denies taxation. Instead, he clearly distinguishes those who mint coins from the One who gives life. Rome has control over Roman money, but God is the giver of life. So give back to Rome what they control and give to God your life.

In Advent, as we hope in the coming Light, let us give ourselves to the important things. Let us give ourselves to the God of life in order that we might shine like stars in this dark world.

What have you given yourself to this week?

=========================== **PRAYER** ===========================

Lord Jesus, the Advent candle burns with hope.
Its faint glow serves to remind us that we share the
hope the prophets held—that you will return in time.
We long for the day your light will pierce the darkness.

———————————————— AMEN ————————————————

ADVENT SEASON • WEEK TWO

THE ONE
A Devotional Reflection Based on Mark 1:1–8

Instead of having angels, shepherds, or wise men prepare us for Christmas, the gospel of Mark gives us a weather-beaten prophet wearing camel-hair clothes and a leather belt. This desert prophet, known as John the Baptizer, is the first person Mark wants us to meet as he gets ready to tell us the good news. Mark spends no time at all on the stories of the first Christmas. There is simply this announcement: "The beginning of the good news of Jesus Christ, the Son of God" (v. 1, NRSV). The rugged baptizing preacher is the messenger, and his message is about Christ, the embodiment of this good news. Jesus is the Son of God, and the story that unfolds is his story.

Mark does not get to Jesus right away because he wants us to pay attention to John's preaching. Standing knee deep in the turbid waters of the Jordan River, John calls out to the crowds gathered along its banks, "Get ready! 'Prepare the way of the Lord, make his paths straight' [v. 3, NRSV]." John's message is an urgent call to make our relationship with God our first priority. We are to do this by confessing our sin and turning in repentance toward God so that we are ready when the Messiah shows up. We need to be listening. The prophetic word asks us to abandon our frantic holiday preparations—the gift-buying frenzy at malls and department stores and other activities that so drain people during the days leading up to Christmas that *the* day itself finds them spiritually empty and emotionally spent. Instead, we are to listen to the voice crying in the wilderness of our exhausting celebrations.

With no baby Jesus, no stable, no star in the sky, Mark launches his good news with these sparse sentences about the baptizing John and his message about *the One who is coming*. Here is another Advent word that urges restraint in rushing to Bethlehem too early. The good news first wants us to pay attention to this straightforward statement about getting things right with God. John wants us prepared to meet the Christ who brings God's peace and goodwill to the world—peace that comes when we are reconciled to God and with each other.

Here is why people from all over Judea went out to listen to John, why they traveled far from the centers of power and set aside their daily tasks. They were spiritually hungry. They had given up on oppressive religious systems and were tired of stale remarks and shallow, sentimental talk about God. They came to this broad bend in the Jordan River, to the edge of the desert, to meet the Baptizer and to find out if their search for God would turn up anything interesting.

Clearly John's message is a great Christmas message after all— the God people have been seeking is about to come looking for them. Because he is coming, they need to be ready, and the only way to be ready is to declare publically their confession by the baptism of repentance. Then they will hear in response to their seeking: "The one who is more powerful than I is coming after me; I am not worthy to stoop down and untie the thong of his sandals. I have baptized you with water; but he will baptize you with the Holy Spirit" (v. 7, NRSV).

John knows that what *he* is doing is not about himself. His is the voice in the wilderness of our busy and chaotic lives, calling us to get ready for the great coming of God—to prepare our hearts to receive the One who is Wonderful Counselor, Mighty God, Everlasting Father, Prince of Peace. The baptism of repentance John announces to the crowds calls them not only to confess their sins but also to turn *away* from them and turn *toward* God. Only then will the people be ready for what God is about to do.

As we take these next steps along the road toward Bethlehem, we stop long enough at the Jordan to hear from John the Baptist. The scriptures that illuminate the mysteries of Christmas urge us to find this place of confession *and* repentance. As we stand there in the desert heat on the riverbank with the crowd, we are anxiously looking around for the One about whom John is talking. Advent warns us that he is not only coming again but is indeed already among us. So we listen to this desert prophet, the Baptizer, the most unlikely of Christmas characters. We get on with the business of straightening things up in our lives and rise from the waters of our baptism of repentance at peace with God—only to discover that the One who is coming is already here.

PREPARE FOR WORSHIP—THE BETHLEHEM CANDLE
Second Sunday of Advent

The second candle of Advent is the Bethlehem candle, which symbolizes love. Over two thousand years ago in the small town of Bethlehem God's chosen one, Jesus, was born. This baby was a sign of God's unfailing love for his people, Israel, and the whole world. As we prepare to celebrate the birth of Jesus, we also wait for the return of the Son of God, who will shine light into the darkness. While we wait, we participate as signs of God's unfailing love. Today we are called to love with the Light.

MONDAY • LOVE WITH THE LIGHT

Show me your ways, O Lord, teach me your paths;
guide me in your truth and teach me, for you are
God my Savior, and my hope is in you all day long.

—— PSALM 25:4–5 ——

 ## CONNECTION

LOVE

This week two flames appear on the Advent wreath, hope and love. Our anticipation begins to build knowing that the Light of God is increasing and the darkness is decreasing. The brightness of the two flames is a sign that together as the family of God we are beacons of love to the chaotic seas of our world as we prepare to celebrate the coming of our Savior.

God's love for us began before we were ever created. In the midst of God—Father, Son, and Holy Spirit—love is eternal and infinite. All things were created out of God's love. So God called all creation good.

Humans marred the goodness of creation by rejecting God. Our angry "No!" to God didn't sidetrack his plan. In love, God came into this world and pursued us to the point of death, even death on a cross. It is the love of God that illuminates our world in Christ Jesus, our Lord, and fills us with the responsibility to love our neighbor as ourselves.

We are now entering a time of remembrance and preparation. As we prepare to remember the first coming of Jesus, God's chosen one, we retell the story of God's good news of love to the world. And as we prepare by remembering what Jesus taught about his return, we are moved to go out into the world to witness to our neighbors and family about the Light of the World.

In worship, we lit the Bethlehem candle that symbolizes love. We're sent to look for and live as signs of love in the world. The aim for us this week is to search for the light of love in others, in ourselves, and in the world.

FAMILY DEVOTIONS
Light the Advent candles • Gospel Reading: Matt. 22:23-33

EMBRACE THE LOVE OF GOD

Advent is a season for us to be fully present by remembering the past (the first advent) and looking forward to the future (the second advent). It is a time for us to embrace the reality that the church is an ancient-future people.

Our hope for the future, at the second advent, is the resurrection of the dead. This is an ancient hope. In verses 31-32 of today's gospel reading Jesus reveals to us that the living God is still in a covenant relationship with the fathers of the faith who died long ago. And if God is in relationship with them, then they, too, must be living and not dead. So our hope in the resurrection rests upon God's love for us.

During Advent we are called to remember the love of God. Because of his love, God sent his only Son into the world so that all might be saved from death. We also look forward with confidence in God's love that on the day the Son of God comes again we will be like him, raised from death to life. Advent is a time when we are invited to embrace the love of the living God by remembering and hoping.

===== **PRAYER** =====

Light of light, we humbly pray, shine upon your world today. Break the gloom of our dark night and fill our souls with love and light.[6]

•————————— **AMEN** —————————•

===== **DAILY PSALM** =====

Your love, O LORD, reaches to the heavens, your faithfulness to the skies. Your righteousness is like the mighty mountains, your justice like the great deep. O LORD, you preserve both man and beast. How priceless is your unfailing love! Both high and low among men find refuge in the shadow of your wings.

———————————— **PSALM 36:5–7** ————————————

 CONNECTION

LOVE PROJECTS

Are you ready to practice being the light of love?

Huddle the family and read through these ideas for living out the love of God this week. If these ideas are not a good fit, feel free to try something else or continue a family tradition that is already an act of Christian love.

CRISIS CARE
One way to spread the love of God to the world is to provide for emergencies and natural disasters. Check out this Web site for instructions on how to prepare crisis care kits and partner with an agency that uses them in disaster relief efforts: http://www.ncm.org/act/disasterresponse/cck/.

EXTEND YOUR FAMILY
Take your family to an assisted living home for a visit. Your only agenda is to find someone who you can listen to and share your life with.

SPREAD THE WARMTH
Look through your closets and storage and get out all the gently used clothes you don't wear. Then donate them to a clothing bank or organization that will give them away to others who need warm clothes this year.

LOVE NOTES

Nothing says love like a good old handwritten note. Get your family together and think of some people in your church family whom you want to encourage. Write a message or draw a picture to let them know you appreciate them.

FAMILY DEVOTIONS
Light the Advent candles • Gospel Reading: Matt. 22:34-46

FREE TO LOVE

Yesterday's gospel reading leads us to a place of freedom. To embrace the love of the living God means we have accepted the reality that there is no place in all of creation, both visible and invisible, that will "separate us from the love of God that is in Christ Jesus our Lord" (Rom. 8:39). In our gospel reading today we read the familiar and often repeated greatest commandments: "Love the Lord your God with all your heart and with all your soul and with all your mind," and "love your neighbor as yourself" (Matt. 22:37, 39). The conclusion is that we are now free to love God with our whole being and to love our neighbor as we are loved by God.

Embracing God's love sets us on the path of living like Jesus. We are called into a radical love relationship with God that overflows to those in need around us. And as we love those in need, it fuels our love for God. It is a wild cycle of love directed by the Holy Spirit toward that great day when the Son of God returns and reunites us and all creation to God the Father.

This Advent season we are invited to accept God's love offered to us in Jesus Christ. We are also invited to journey deep into that love by giving all of ourselves to loving God and loving our neighbor. So let us prepare ourselves this Advent season by loving through the Light of the World.

═══════════ **PRAYER** ═══════════

Redeemer, come, with us abide. Our hearts to you we open wide. Let us your inner presence feel; your grace and love in us reveal.[7]

•─────────── **AMEN** ───────────•

=== **DAILY PSALM** ===

*I have chosen the way of truth; I have set my heart
on your laws. I hold fast to your statutes, O LORD;
do not let me be put to shame. I run in the path of
your commands, for you have set my heart free.*

—— **PSALM 119:30–32** ——

 CONNECTION

THE SYMBOLISM OF THE ADVENT WREATH

The green of the Advent wreath is a symbol of life and renewal. The first sign of renewal we discover in God's story is with Abraham. God made a covenant or promise that he would bless Abraham with land, descendants, and the calling to bless the world.

Another sign of life and renewal experienced by God's promised people was in the Exodus. The people of God had been enslaved in Egypt for hundreds of years. They cried out to God for help, and he heard their cry. God sent Moses to tell Pharaoh to let God's people go so they could worship him. When Pharaoh refused, God miraculously freed his people and led them out of Egypt to new life.

God continued to lead his people toward renewal and life by providing them with a way of life. God gave the Ten Commandments to Israel so they could be blessed and be a blessing to the world. God also gave Israel the land promised to their forefather Abraham. But Israel started a dangerous pattern of living and would not follow God's way of life. So they would experience destruction and cry out to God to rescue them.

God was faithful to his promise and lovingly rescued Israel over and over again. God's patience and love taught Israel to hope in God.

We are called to embrace that same lesson Israel learned so long ago. As we wait for the coming of the Light of the World, we're invited to embrace the God of love as our hope.

FAMILY DEVOTIONS
Light the Advent candles • Gospel Reading: Matt. 23:1-12

WHAT DO WE LOVE?

During Advent the world pounds at the door to our hearts through commercials and advertisements. Images of excited children receiving gifts and glowing faces of family members as they bask in the joy of giving make this time of year seem unreal. So what do we love so much that makes everyone happier at this time of year?

Jesus suggests one possible answer in our gospel reading. In his warning to both the religious leaders and his disciples, Jesus observes that we love to receive honor from others (v. 5). When what we do is done only to receive praise, love, and respect from others, then our love is misplaced.

What if more of our giving was done in secret this year? What if we didn't seek approval or recognition for our gifts? Would people still be as happy?

The scripture reminds us that we are to love the way a family loves. The image is one of a brother or sister caring for a family member simply because he or she is part of the family. It also reminds us that we should give as if we are only trying to impress our Father "who sees what is done in secret" (6:4). Prepare for the advent of Jesus by loving and caring for others with no expectations.

=== **PRAYER** ===

Prepare my heart, Lord Jesus, turn not
from me aside, and grant that I receive you
this blessed Adventide.[8]

—————— AMEN ——————

37

THURSDAY • LOVE WITH THE LIGHT

*Delight yourself in the L*ORD *and he will give you the desires of your heart. Commit your way to the L*ORD*; trust in him and he will do this: He will make your righteousness shine like the dawn, the justice of your cause like the noonday sun. Be still before the L*ORD *and wait patiently for him.*

———— PSALM 37:4–7 ————

 ## CONNECTION

FAMILY STORIES OF LOVE

Today, connect your family stories to this week's Advent theme of love. Think about how you can begin sharing your family stories of loving God and neighbor.

ENGAGE

Idea 1: Get on Facebook or pull out the photo albums. Take a trip down memory lane and share some family stories of love.

Idea 2: Ask everyone in the family to find one possession that helps him or her feel loved. Invite each one to share it and to tell why the object is a reminder of love.

DISCUSS
• What does love feel like?
• When have you felt loved by family and friends?
• When have you experienced God's love in a tangible way?

 **FAMILY DEVOTIONS**
Light the Advent candles • Gospel Reading: Matt. 23:13-26

ACTS OF LOVE

Being busy seems to be the norm for most people during Advent. There are school assignments to complete and tests to take. There are more activities with friends and family. There are deadlines to meet before vacation can begin. All of this activity makes Advent less about preparing and anticipating and more about getting things done and rushing around.

Our gospel reading today asks us to reflect on our priorities once again. If all our preparation for Advent is simply a checking off of religious duties—church attendance, Christmas play practice, devotional time, scripture reading, and so on—we'll never enter the experience of Advent. It will be as though we "strain[ed] out a gnat but swallow[ed] a camel" (v. 24). We'll do the small things and miss the big picture.

The experience of Advent is to prepare and anticipate the coming of the Light of the World by practicing justice, mercy, and faithfulness in our families and daily activities. We enter that experience by focusing on God, who has come and will come again. That focus will reset our priorities.

Talk about your family priorities and decide what will lead you to focus on the Light of Advent.

=================== **PRAYER** ===================

Come, O long expected Jesus, born to set your people free. From our fears and sins release us, and let us find our rest in you.[9]

——————— AMEN ———————

=== **DAILY PSALM** ===

Let your face shine on your servant;
save me in your unfailing love.

———————— PSALM 31:16 ————————

 CONNECTION

SYMBOLS OF THE SEASON—
EVERGREEN TREE

The evergreen tree is a popular symbol of Christmas both inside and outside the church. The evergreen tree is rich and diverse in symbolism. The evergreen is a symbol of the eternal life of God and the continual renewal he brings to us. To some the tree represents the cross, with branches stretching from the middle and the top pointing to the heavens. The decorations and lights on the evergreen symbolize the celebration of the long-anticipated coming of the chosen one of God, Jesus. Whatever symbolic meaning you choose to embrace, allow it to be a connection to your preparation for the coming of the Light of the World.

LOVE IS PATIENT

Patience has its limits. We can only handle so much stress. During this time of the year it isn't uncommon for people to reach their limits and become impatient.

Today we are given a beautiful picture of God. We are to imagine God with a deep desire to bring all of his chosen people together like "a hen gathers her chicks under her wings" (v. 37). We are invited to imagine God working all around the world to guide and direct all of his people back to him in a loving and gentle way. God longs for us to know the safety of his presence.

God was rejected by his chosen people. Time and again God attempted to guide and direct them, but they quickly turned away. They refused to be gathered under the protection of God's wings.

The patience of God endured for thousands of years, and it continues to endure. God still longs to gather his chosen people together. When the Light of the World comes again, God will complete the work he started. But God is patient because that day will also mean some people will not be prepared and so will be judged accordingly. Advent reminds us that we are given time to prepare for God's return because God is patient and wants no one to perish (see 2 Pet. 3:9).

It is comforting to know that God is not like us. Our patience has a limit of seconds, hours, or days. The limits of God's patience are unknown because his love endures forever.

=== **PRAYER** ===

Soon I shall see you as you are, the Light that came to me; I'll behold the brightness of your face, throughout eternity.[10]

—— AMEN ——

41

SATURDAY • LOVE WITH THE LIGHT

DAILY PSALM

Send forth your light and your truth, let them guide me; let them bring me to your holy mountain, to the place where you dwell.

— PSALM 43:3 —

 CONNECTION

REFLECT ON THE WEEK TOGETHER

• Where did you see God at work in your week?

• What did you learn about love this week?

• How did you practice being God's love to other people?

• Is there a time where you experienced God's love this week?

FAMILY DEVOTIONS
Light the Advent candles • Gospel Reading: Matt. 24:1-14

THE REACH OF GOD'S LOVE

It's captivating to imagine the whole world hearing the good news of Jesus Christ. The task seems impossible from a human perspective. But thanks to God we do not put our trust in a human perspective. Rather, God's perspective is that the performance and proclamation of his good news to the world will be done before Jesus returns.

It is hard to deny that the love of God is endless when you think about God's perspective. God has waited patiently for thousands of years as he has guided the church in his mission. God has pushed and prodded his people to love and announce the love of God to their neighbors even through the darkest periods of history. Through it all, God, in his endless love, is still using the church and still guiding his people to be his hands and feet to a broken world.

The preparation for Advent includes our recognition that we are called to preach the good news to the world. We are to love our neighbors as ourselves so they can understand what we mean when we tell them about the love of God in Christ Jesus, our Lord. Let us participate by sharing the good news of our Lord with our families and friends today.

=================== **PRAYER** ===================

Lord Jesus, the Advent candle burns with love. Its flame is warm and inviting, unlike the little town of Bethlehem, where your love first came shining. We long for the day your light will pierce the darkness.

●————————————————— AMEN —————————————————●

SUNDAY • JOY FOR THE LIGHT

ADVENT SEASON • WEEK THREE

THE VOICE
A Devotional Reflection Based on John 1:6-8, 19-28

John the Baptist—again?! That's right—again! We can't continue our journey to Bethlehem without giving him some more attention, although he doesn't want our attention. He wants all our attention on the One who is coming after him. At the Jordan River this strange-looking prophet announces to the gathered crowd the coming of the Messiah, who will usher in the kingdom of God. And nearby a black-robed committee of religious leaders stands listening as the Baptist preaches a baptism of repentance and forgiveness of sin.

The Baptist, squinting in the bright sunlight, locks eyes with the committee. They want to know who he thinks he is. Right away, John lets them know who he is not: "He confessed and did not deny it, but confessed, '*I am not the Messiah*'" (v. 20, NRSV, emphasis added). Raising his arms, he loudly declares, "I am the *voice* of one crying out in the wilderness, 'Make straight the way of the Lord'" (v. 23, NRSV, emphasis added). The religious committee is not amused. This wilderness baptizer is not the Messiah, nor does he seem to be any of the expected forerunners of the Messiah—a reappearing Elijah or prophet like Moses. So who is he? John will not let them trap him into making any outlandish claims.

Remember, John knows who he is. He is a *voice*—he is *not* the Christ. His words echo the ancient prophet Isaiah: "A voice cries out: 'In the wilderness prepare the way of the LORD, make straight in the desert a highway for our God'" (Isa. 40:3, NRSV). John's role is simply to get things ready. Set the table, and step aside for the Host. Be a good best man without upstaging the Bridegroom.

So now that we have heard this voice preparing us for the Messiah's coming, what do we do next? How do we straighten the paths and make it easy for the Messiah to enter into all the places we live, work, and play? Even though he is not Elijah, nor the prophet like Moses, John's message recalls the recurring themes of Israel's prophets. Do you remember our gospel reading for the first Sunday of Advent? It was about hope and getting ready for Christ's sudden appearance. And the reading for the second Sunday? It was about the peace that comforts our hearts after we confess our sins and repent. Only after we sincerely repent can we find peace with God.

We find on this third Advent Sunday that John has something startling to say to his questioners: "Among you stands one whom you do not know" (John 1:26, NRSV). The Promised One *already* stands among us? Certainly he will come at the end of all things when the kingdoms of this world will become the kingdom of our Lord and of his Christ. It is also true that we are on our way to Bethlehem to remember that moment when he first came among us as the swaddled Immanuel.

Yet before we approach the manger where God appears as divine mercy incarnate, we need to know that the Messiah's coming is *very* much in the present tense. Christ is here right now. Close-minded religious types do not know him yet. Political leaders have yet to be introduced. Even John is scanning the crowd looking for him, because he knows, after all, that he is just a *voice*. He is only the announcer telling us about the star player. Actually, John knows he is getting ready for his *biggest* announcement, the purpose for which he was born so miraculously to Elizabeth and Zechariah. As the *voice*, he will proclaim something strong and deeply moving. With boldness and confidence, John will introduce the Christ: "Here is the Lamb of God who takes away the sin of the world!" (v. 29, NRSV).

As we draw closer to Christmas, we see the necessity of what we have explored each Sunday of Advent. No hope-filled urgency in our preparation? No true Christmas. No sincere repentance? No true Christmas. No sacrificial Lamb? No true Christmas.

These are the Advent messages that illuminate the mysteries of this holy season as we journey to Bethlehem. The "full of grace and truth" Babe, the "Word made flesh" Messiah, is both our destination and our companion on the journey. We dare not get any closer to the Christmas crib until we acknowledge that the Messiah is already the One who stands among us. Now we are ready for the really big announcement—through God's angelic messenger—shocking awake a sleepy world: "Do not be afraid; for see—*I am bringing you good news of great joy for all the people*: to you is born this day in the city of David a Savior, who is the Messiah, the Lord" (Luke 2:10-11, NRSV, emphasis added).

PREPARE FOR WORSHIP—THE SHEPHERDS' CANDLE
Third Sunday of Advent

The third candle of Advent is the shepherds' candle, which symbolizes joy. The shepherds were the first of God's people to receive the news of Jesus' birth, and it filled them with overflowing joy. They ran around praising God for what they saw and heard. Our anticipation for what is to come turns to great joy because we know God will come again to judge the darkness and spread the light of joy throughout the whole world. Today we are called to experience and share joy for the Light.

=========== **DAILY PSALM** ===========

We have heard with our ears, O God; our fathers have told us what you did in their days, in days long ago. With your hand you drove out the nations and planted our fathers; you crushed the peoples and made our fathers flourish. It was not by their sword that they won the land, nor did their arm bring them victory. It was your right hand, your arm, and the light of your face, for you loved them.

———————————— **PSALM 44:1–3** ————————————

 CONNECTION

JOY

Three lights dance on top of the candles, illuminating our Advent journey. Hope and love are now accompanied by great joy as we anticipate the celebration of the birth of the Son of God that is only two weeks away. God's presence in our activities and prayers is the reason for our deep sense of joy.

Christian joy is greater than the joy the world offers. The world offers us joy in sleek-designed gadgets wrapped in shiny paper. The world's joy lasts only for a time. Christian joy flows from memories of all the ways God was present in the impossible moments of life. Money from an unknown donor, survival from a severe illness or accident, and an encouraging word in a time of despair—all are examples of God's presence in life's impossible moments. Add all those stories to the countless stories from the time of Genesis to today, and you have reason for great joy. So let's throw all of our efforts into joyfully preparing for the celebration of our Savior, who has come and will come again.

In worship, we lit the shepherds' candle, which symbolizes joy. We're sent to watch for and live as signs of joy in the world. The aim for us this week is to search for the light of joy in others, in ourselves, and in the world.

WE CAN'T MISS THE JOY

Have you ever missed going to a party because you got the time wrong? You set aside time out of your week for it. You buy stuff in advance. You spend time getting ready. Then you show up and everyone is leaving.

Now, what do you think it was like preparing for Jesus' return in the early church? There were probably people who had heard Jesus teach and saw him after his resurrection. Can you imagine their passion for following Jesus' teaching? Can you imagine their desire to tell others about who Jesus was and what he did? Can you imagine how they longed and prayed for Jesus' return? Now imagine what would happen if a person claimed to have seen Jesus return. How disappointed would everyone be once they discovered the claim to be untrue?

It must have filled the original hearers of Matthew's gospel with great joy to hear that the return of the Son of Man would not be some small event. With people spreading rumors about Jesus' return, it was good news to hear that his return would be a worldwide event. Our passage describes the return of Jesus as lightning that is visible from east to west (v. 27). The second advent will be so dramatic that no one will be able to miss it.

We can joyously prepare for the second advent knowing that it won't be something we can miss.

=== **PRAYER** ===

You come, the wide world's King. You come, the true heart's Friend. New gladness to begin, and ancient wrong to end. You come, to fill with light the weary waiting eye. We lift our heads and rejoice—redemption is nearby.[11]

—— AMEN ——

=== **DAILY PSALM** ===

God has ascended amid shouts of joy, the LORD amid the sounding of trumpets. Sing praises to God, sing praises; sing praises to our King, sing praises.

— **PSALM 47:5–6** —

 CONNECTION

JOY PROJECTS

Are you ready to practice being the light of joy?

This week should be fun for everyone. Gather your friends and family together. Look over the ideas for spreading the joy of the Lord to your neighbors. You can try any of these ideas or feel free to use your own.

EXTEND YOUR FAMILY
Here is an organization that will allow you to support a child in a developing country. Check out the site and think about extending your family through the joy of child sponsorship: http://www.ncm.org/act/childdevelopment/.

CHRISTMAS CAROLING
If caroling is already a family tradition in your church or with your extended family, then continue it. If not, then consider caroling to your neighbors this year.

HANDMADE GIFTS
As a family, instead of spending money on Christmas presents this year consider making them. Making something by hand can be a true joy.

JOY BOX
Buy a small storage box or decorate a shoebox. Then place it in a high-traffic area of your home along with note cards and paper.

When the mood hits you, write down a joyous memory, story, or thought and drop it in the box. You can do this for the next twelve months so that by the next Advent season you can share all the joyful memories God provided over the year.

FAMILY DEVOTIONS
Light the Advent candles • Gospel Reading: Matt. 24:32-44

JOY IN TRUSTING

Not knowing when Jesus will return should not produce fear in us. Not knowing keeps us from unnecessary worry. What is important is that Jesus said he would return, and he teaches us that his words will never pass away (v. 35). We can trust Jesus that what he says will happen.

We should respond by being watchful, not out of a fear of punishment, but because we are excited about the Lord coming back. We also know that being watchful means we are to follow the teachings of Jesus because his words will never pass away.

What a joy it is to trust God with our future. Followers of Jesus do not need to worry about the details of God's future actions. We can simply trust him like children trusting a parent to care for us each day. So let's keep being watchful and allow the anticipation of Jesus' return to fill us with joy.

=== PRAYER ===

Christ, whose glory fills the skies; Christ, the true, the only Light—Sun of Righteousness, arise and triumph over the shades of night. Dayspring from on high, come near. Day-star, in my heart appear.[12]

—— AMEN ——

DAILY PSALM

This is the fate of those who trust in themselves, and of their followers, who approve their sayings. Like sheep they are destined for the grave, and death will feed on them. The upright will rule over them in the morning; their forms will decay in the grave, far from their princely mansions. But God will redeem my life from the grave; he will surely take me to himself.

— PSALM 49:13–15 —

 CONNECTION

THE SYMBOLISM OF THE ADVENT WREATH

The four outer candles symbolize a period of waiting. Within the tradition of the church some believe that the four candles represent the four hundred years of silence from God between the last revelations of the Old Testament and the coming of Christ.

Many things happened to God's people before those years of silence. Israel's unfaithful way of life with God led to periods of waiting. God allowed them to experience the destructive consequences of their sinful choices. They would lose battles with other nations and then cry out to God, and he would rescue them. Years of unfaithfulness under the leadership of evil kings, corrupt priests, and pandering prophets increased the punishment for Israel's sin. First, the nation was split into two separate kingdoms. Then the divided nation was defeated and dragged into exile in Babylon.

Through the years of exile, God spoke to his people through prophets. He taught them that their unfaithfulness caused their downfall. God also revealed to them the promise of the Messiah or chosen one. The belief began to spread that God's chosen one would be sent to rescue Israel from captivity in exile, return them to God's Promised Land, and restore them to a faithful way of life.

God did bring Israel out of captivity and lead them back to the Land of Promise. Yet God's chosen one didn't come, and the waiting in silence began. They waited hundreds of years in anticipation of the day the Messiah would come and fill them with the joy of redemption.

FAMILY DEVOTIONS
Light the Advent candles • Gospel Reading: Matt. 24:45-51

JOY IN FAITHFULNESS

Remember how it felt waiting to open presents on Christmas morning? The anticipation could be overwhelming. Your heart pounded as all your hopes for that one gift flooded your mind. You noticed family members talking, but you couldn't hear anything because you kept wondering what you got.

Our waiting during Advent is like waiting to open presents on Christmas morning. We have images and thoughts about what the day will be like, but we are not sure. We know it will be a huge event. We know that Jesus will bring to completion all he did and said. We know we will be like him if we faithfully follow him. But we also know there will be judgment for those who have chosen not to be faithful to him. It is a day filled with many unknowns, but for us, if we are followers of Jesus, it will be a day of rejoicing because we will be receiving our long-awaited gift.

The parable today reminds us that we should not become lazy in preparing for Jesus' return, even though it seems as if it is taking a long time. If we remain faithful until the end, it will be a good day for us.

Preparing for the celebration of the first advent reminds us of the joy that will be ours if we remain faithful until the second advent.

═══════════ **PRAYER** ═══════════

When next you come with glory, and the world is wrapped in fear, with your mercy you will shield us, and with words of love draw near.[13]

────── AMEN ──────

THURSDAY •

DAILY PSALM

Sacrifice and offering you did not desire,
but my ears you have pierced; burnt offerings
and sin offerings you did not require. Then I said,
"Here I am, I have come—it is written about me
in the scroll. I desire to do your will, O my God;
your law is within my heart."

—— PSALM 40:6–8 ——

 CONNECTION

FAMILY STORIES OF JOY

Today, connect your family stories to this week's Advent theme of joy. Think about how you can begin sharing your family stories of joy in God.

ENGAGE

Idea 1: Pick a fun game to play as a family and let the conversation start from there and spread to talking about stories of joy.

Idea 2: Ask everyone in the family to find one possession that helps him or her feel joyful. Invite each one to share it and to tell why the object is a reminder of joy.

DISCUSS
- What does joy feel like?
- What were some of the joy-filled memories from this year?
- When has God provided or taught you something that filled you with a deep appreciation?

FAMILY DEVOTIONS
Light the Advent candles • Gospel Reading: Matt. 25:1-13

JOY IN WAITING

Have you ever had to wait and watch for something you really wanted? An animal at the zoo to perform? A flower to blossom? A package to arrive? A family member to come home? A gift to be given?

Watching and waiting is not a fun activity for most people. It requires concentration. Concentration means you can be distracted. In other words, if you are keeping watch, then you can't play music, read a magazine, or watch a movie. And the longer you keep watch, the easier it is to get distracted by any little thing. So where is the joy in keeping watch?

The joy is when the thing you had been waiting for arrives. If the object of your waiting is important enough, then all the time in the world will have been worth it. In Advent we practice keeping watch for the One who made the world. The anticipation is building for the day that the Light of the World will appear. Keep watching.

=== **PRAYER** ===

Soon you're coming back to welcome us beyond the starry sky. We will wing our flight to worlds unknown and reign with you on high.[14]

— **AMEN** —

FRIDAY • JOY FOR THE LIGHT

*I long to dwell in your tent forever and take
refuge in the shelter of your wings.*

—————————— PSALM 61:4 ——————————

 CONNECTION

SYMBOLS OF THE SEASON—BELLS

Bells are a symbol of joy and celebration. In the Old Testament bells were hung on the robe of the high priest, and the ringing of the bells quickly became connected to the community's worship. Bells were later used in the church as a way of communicating to the whole community that worship was beginning. As we prepare for the joyous celebration of the coming of the Son of God, let the ringing of the bells fuel our anticipation and excitement to worship.

FAMILY DEVOTIONS
Light the Advent candles • Gospel Reading: Matt. 25:14-30

JOY IN PREPARING

We are given enormous wealth. If we can make this parable slightly allegorical, then the shocking sum of money—think millions of dollars—given to the servants is a symbol of the importance of the kingdom of God. Just like the servants, we are now stewards of God's incredible kingdom and we have the responsibility to extend God's rule. We do this by following the way of the kingdom—loving God and loving our neighbor.

Our preparation for Jesus' return is to be marked by spreading the joyous news of the kingdom of God. This time of year provides unique opportunities to live out the kingdom and tell others about it.

Discuss with your family ways you can spread the joyous news of God's coming to friends and family.

=========================== **PRAYER** ===========================

Lord, you are coming! Let us sound this news
forth from east to west, from south to north.
And when we meet and when we part, let this
be the greeting from our heart.[15]

———————————————————— AMEN ————————————————————

DAILY PSALM

*Where can I go from your Spirit? Where can
I flee from your presence? If I go up to the
heavens, you are there; if I make my bed in
the depths, you are there. If I rise on the wings
of the dawn, if I settle on the far side of the sea,
even there your hand will guide me, your right
hand will hold me fast.*

— PSALM 139:7–10 —

 ## CONNECTION

REFLECTION ON THE WEEK TOGETHER

• Where did you see God at work in your week?

• What did you learn about joy this week?

• How did you practice spreading the joy of the Lord to others?

• Were there moments in preparing for the coming of Jesus that you experienced joy?

FAMILY DEVOTIONS
Light the Advent candles • Gospel Reading: Matt. 25:31-46

JOY IN CARING FOR THE LEAST

Our world is full of broken systems that ravage people and all creation. In the media we hear about wars raging on year after year and we can become numb to the pain and suffering they cause. We hear repeatedly of global crises, and this news can make us feel at a loss about how to respond.

Preparing for the Light of the World to pierce the darkness means we must care for those in need. Our scripture today tells us that God identifies with the cry of the needy. If we love God, then we will love our neighbor who is in need. Any time we love our neighbor, we love God. In other words, we prepare for the Light of the World by continuing to love God, which means loving our neighbor as ourselves.

The joy is not just that we will be called good and faithful servants on the day of the Lord (see vv. 21, 23). The joy is also found in our being good and faithful servants here and now. We can already enter the joy of the Lord if we follow his way of holy living. We can be children of light now as we care for the least.

Though the brokenness of our world appears vast, the love of God is endless. Let us prepare for the coming of God by participating in his mission to heal our world.

PRAYER

Lord Jesus, the Advent candle burns with joy,
its flicker dancing wildly. Like the shepherds
we rejoice and praise your name loudly. We long
for the day your light will pierce the darkness.

AMEN

ADVENT SEASON • WEEK FOUR

THE GREAT REVERSAL
A Devotional Reflection Based on Luke 1:26-38
(also read Mary's Magnificat—Luke 1:46-55)

Like a play or movie, there are many scenes surrounding the story of Jesus' birth, but the spotlight shines most brilliantly on a humble, whitewashed stucco home in Nazareth. Inside, a young woman named Mary busies herself at a loom. She is weaving fabrics for the new home she and her husband, Joseph, the village carpenter, will share after their marriage.

Suddenly she is aware of a presence and, glancing up, notices a stranger standing before her. Since visitors do not knock in first-century Palestine, but simply step inside and call the name of the person they wish to see, finding someone has entered the home would not ordinarily be a surprise. But in this case, here is someone dressed in white, almost luminescent clothing, whose first words astound her: "Greetings, favored one! The Lord is with you" (v. 28, NRSV).

Six months after the angel Gabriel has told Zechariah and Elizabeth that they will have a child, who becomes John the Baptizer, this same angel now appears to Mary. Although Mary is startled, she displays remarkable self-possession mixed with an understandable amount of fear. Gabriel continues, "Do not be afraid, Mary, for you have found favor with God" (v. 30, NRSV). Then he says, "And now, you will conceive in your womb and bear a son, and you will name him Jesus. He will be great, and will be called the Son of the Most High, and the Lord God will give to him the throne of his ancestor David. He will reign over the house of Jacob forever, and of his kingdom there will be no end" (vv. 31-33, NRSV).

Mary, understanding the immediacy of Gabriel's message, responds, "How can this be, since I am a virgin?" (v. 34, NRSV). She does not doubt what the angel is saying; she just wants more information.

Because Mary believes Gabriel, the angel immediately gives her a beautiful and mysterious answer: "The power of the Most High will overshadow you" (v. 35, NRSV). And then to reward and strengthen her faith further, he tells her that Elizabeth, her aged cousin, is already six months pregnant—another sign to confirm in Mary that nothing is too hard for the Lord.

Perhaps Mary takes a moment to ponder what Gabriel is telling her. Yet as she grasps the implications of the messenger's words to her, she realizes he is waiting for her consent. God never forces the human will. Her answer is typically brief: "Here am I, the servant of the Lord; let it be with me according to your word" (v. 38, NRSV). Identifying herself with the lowest level of society, Mary responds as an obedient servant. Jesus, her Son, will display a similar kind of obedience in his garden prayer— "not my will, but yours be done" (22:42, NRSV)—and so will save the people from their sins.

Mary is alone at this moment. Nobody else knows what she knows, not even Joseph, who has yet to hear from Gabriel. At some point Mary must have felt very lonely and isolated. How would she explain all of this to others—especially Joseph? Yet in Mary's loneliness Immanuel—"God with us"—will make his home. In the kingdom, the lonely know the companionship of God. In fact, the entire Christmas story is about strengthening the weak, freeing the oppressed, and befriending the lonely. God loves and raises these lowly ones up to do his work in the world. He may approach a young teenager, like Mary, or a barren old woman, like Elizabeth. What sets them apart is not just that God calls them but also their response: "Here am I, the servant of the Lord; let it be with me according to your word" (1:38, NRSV).

We are now approaching Bethlehem on our Advent journey. The scriptures that illuminate the mysteries of Christmas challenge our twenty-first-century thinking. The Advent message is a call to embrace a God who identifies with the weak and oppressed, the empty and lonely, the outcast and vulnerable. We confess with Mary—in faith, hope, and love—that "the Mighty One has done great things for me" (v. 49, NRSV). We acknowledge that the powers of this world are not the powers that matter most and that the God of love is the great leveler of all humanity. It is he who brings down the exalted and lifts up the lowly. Our challenge is to view the world through God's eyes. We are to order our values as he does, and that means we, too, are to identify with the weak, the oppressed, and the lonely.

As we draw close to Bethlehem, we are hearing the strains of Mary's magnificent Magnificat—that God does much of his work with powerless people whose lives the world considers impossible. Yet the message is not mainly about social justice, economic equality, or social status. Rather, it is a word about God bringing salvation to *all* those who have come to a dead end in life and recognize their helplessness. God has not forgotten his promise to show them his mercy. Behold, Love has appeared, curled up quietly in the womb of our lonely world!

PREPARE FOR WORSHIP—THE ANGELS' CANDLE
Fourth Sunday of Advent

The fourth candle of Advent is the angels' candle, which symbolizes peace. On the night Jesus was born, angels, messengers sent from God, appeared to some Jewish shepherds with a message of peace. They sang, "Glory to God in the highest, and on earth peace to men on whom his favor rests" (Luke 2:14). Jesus' birth was the light of peace that pierced the darkness. We continue to hope for the return of the Light of the World so that peace can shine everywhere. Today we are called to seek for peace through the Light.

MONDAY •

=== **DAILY PSALM** ===

My soul finds rest in God alone; my salvation comes from him. He alone is my rock and my salvation; he is my fortress, I will never be shaken.

———— PSALM 62:1–2 ————

 CONNECTION

PEACE

The radiance of four candles burning is a sign that the time is near. All of our preparation—through actions of love, prayers of hope, and stories of joy—done through the guidance of the Holy Spirit, is leading us into the way of peace.

The peace that is often talked about on the news is an absence of violence. If a peace treaty is signed, then it is assumed that two countries or parties have stopped fighting. The image of the peace treaty also teaches us that peace is a temporary state in our world. We begin to assume that war and violence is the normal way for disagreements to be settled.

When we turn to Scriptures, we get a different picture of peace. God's action of peace is not just an absence of violence but actually a movement to restore harmony between the many relationships of creation and humanity. The image of God's peace in Scripture is one where war is no longer a part of our world. Nations will turn their instruments of war into tools for the care of creation (see Isa. 2:4). Everyone will have food, and fear will be absent from our hearts. God's peace is a wholeness of relationships throughout all creation. This is the peace we hope for at the second coming of our Lord. It is the peace we are called to practice now.

In worship, we lit the angels' candle, which symbolizes peace. We're sent to seek out and live as signs of peace in the world. The aim for us this week is to search for the light of peace in others, in ourselves, and in the world.

ELIZABETH RECEIVES GOD'S PEACE

The celebration of the birth of God's Son is a week away. Our anticipation is building as the lights of Advent burn bright. Yet, in all of the joy of preparing for the return of Jesus there are some of us who are dealing with some impossible situations. The realities of loneliness, depression, and loss can be magnified during this time of year. All these feelings can lead to a sense of hopelessness at a time when everyone else is celebrating.

Elizabeth's story becomes good news for many during Advent. We are told she was a righteous woman and part of a family of Jewish priests. We are also told she was barren, not able to have children. Being barren in her day was a sign to everyone that God's blessing was not with her. We are told she felt disgraced in her community (v. 25). Disgraced and disconnected, she lived in an impossible situation for years.

The good news for Elizabeth was that God chose to give her peace. Her husband was told that she would give birth to a son, John, who would be used by God to prepare the people of God for the coming of the Lord. She became pregnant as predicted, and she gave praise to God. She said, "He has shown his favor and taken away my disgrace among the people" (v. 25).

An impossible situation was transformed by God. He restored relationships and gave Elizabeth the new life of a child. God brought wholeness to Elizabeth, and God can bring wholeness to our lives today. May God's peace shine into your life at the coming of Jesus Christ through the power of the Spirit.

=== PRAYER ===

Let all the world in one accord shout for your coming, Lord. We praise you, Prince of heavenly birth, who brings peace to all the earth.[16]

—— AMEN ——

DAILY PSALM

Praise the LORD, all you nations; extol him, all you peoples. For great is his love toward us, and the faithfulness of the LORD endures forever. Praise the LORD.

PSALM 117:1-2

 CONNECTION

PEACE PROJECTS

Are you ready to practice being the light of peace?

The celebration of Christmas is a week away. Get the group together again and figure out a way to spread the bright light of peace to your community this week. As usual, here are some ideas to get you thinking.

PRAYER WALK – Get the family and friends together to do a prayer walk for peace in your neighborhood. Pray for safe homes, safe places for children to play, protection for law enforcement, and peace among neighbors.

A PSALM OF PEACE – Write a psalm of peace for your family. Read through several psalms as a guide to your writing, and then think of all the ways God has brought peace to your family, church family, community, and the world. Put it all together into a psalm that your family can use for devotional times.

OPEN UP THE CHURCH – If your church is in a central area of your community, think about opening the church up on the weekend. Let the community know it will be a safe place where you can get warm, free drinks, and good conversation.

LOOSE CHANGE TO LOOSEN CHAINS – Peace comes at a cost for modern-day slaves. Check out this Web site to find out how you can partner with an international agency working to free slaves today: http://www.ijm.org/getinvolved/youth.

FAMILY DEVOTIONS
Light the Advent candles • Gospel Reading: Luke 1:26-38

GABRIEL SPEAKS GOD'S PEACE

Gabriel, an angel or messenger of God, is sent to deliver news once again. Gabriel is a sign of God's presence for us. When we see Gabriel appear in the story, we feel the same kind of awe and fear as Mary in today's story and Zechariah in yesterday's story. While it may be true that seeing Gabriel caused fear, we can also assume that the appearing of a messenger of God also comes with an overwhelming sense of God's presence. We are invited to recognize God, who inspires a feeling of awe, in the midst of this holy announcement.

The messenger of God speaks to calm our fears saying, "Do not be afraid" (v. 30). We can be at peace knowing that God is at work. We can be filled with joy knowing that the time is right and that God has broken the years of silence. We can be wrapped in love realizing that a humble servant is found who will allow God to work out his salvation. We can be consumed with hope at the beacon of truth: "Nothing is impossible with God" (v. 37).

The messenger of God once again speaks to calm our fears in Advent. To the one who fears that our preparations are meaningless, the messenger proclaims, "Don't be afraid. The Son of the Most High is coming." To the one who fears the darkness in the world, the messenger proclaims, "Fear not. The Light will dawn." So let us recognize God in the midst of this holy announcement and respond with the cry of the faithful: "Come, Lord Jesus!"

=== PRAYER ===

Still we wait for your appearing. Life and joy your beams impart, chasing all our fears, and cheering every unenlightened heart. By your all-redeeming merit every burdened soul release; every weary, wandering spirit guide into your perfect peace.[17]

— AMEN —

DAILY PSALM

*Praise be to the LORD God, the God of Israel,
who alone does marvelous deeds. Praise be to his
glorious name forever; may the whole earth be
filled with his glory. Amen and Amen.*

———— PSALM 72:18–19 ————

 CONNECTION

THE SYMBOLISM OF THE ADVENT WREATH

The light from the flames of the Advent wreath symbolizes the light of God. When the time was right, God's light pierced our dark world in the birth of the Messiah, Jesus.

The people of Israel had been waiting for hundreds of years for God's Messiah to come. They lived in the Promised Land of Abraham but were ruled by a foreign nation called Rome. They longed for the Messiah to save them from Rome so they could experience the fulfillment of all of God's promises.

Finally, God decided the right time had come. So God sent an angel to a young woman named Mary. The angel announced that God had chosen Mary to be the mother of the Son of God. Mary accepted the great responsibility saying, "I am the Lord's servant. . . . May it be to me as you have said" (Luke 1:38).

And so now we stand in the place of Mary. We, the church, are to carry God's light into the world. As the body of Christ we are to live out the way of peace, because we know that God is in control of this world and that he will set all things right at the coming of the Lord Jesus.

MARY PRAISES GOD'S PEACE

Mary is a real person with real fears. When we first encounter Mary in Luke's gospel, she is given a shocking greeting. The greeting disturbs her, and the angel must speak words of peace to her. As the messenger of God continues to reveal God's plan for her to carry the promised Son, she is left wondering how all of it can happen. What we get from these opening scenes with Mary is that she is an actual person with genuine fears, hopes, questions, and desires.

The extraordinary grace-filled action Mary takes is to accept God's plan for her. Her response is contrasted with Zechariah's doubt-filled response. This makes Mary our example of faithfulness in preparing for the coming of the Lord. We are invited to trust that as we continue to prepare for the return of the Lord, God's plan will bring peace to our world.

In our gospel reading today, Mary leads us into praising God's peace. Her song teaches us that, like her, we are pulled into God's ancient story of bringing peace into the world through his chosen people. She sings for us the magnitude of what God is doing and reminds us that all of our preparation in Advent is a part of the salvation story of God.

===== **PRAYER** =====

*O Lord, you come in mercy; O Lord, you
come in might. You come to end the evil.
You come to crown the right. Bring your light
that has no evening—that knows neither moon
nor sun. Shine your light so new and golden,
your light, the only one.*[18]

———— AMEN ————

THURSDAY •

DAILY PSALM

Blessed is he whose help is the God of Jacob, whose hope is in the LORD his God, the Maker of heaven and earth, the sea, and everything in them—the LORD, who remains faithful forever. He upholds the cause of the oppressed and gives food to the hungry. The LORD sets prisoners free, the LORD gives sight to the blind, the LORD lifts up those who are bowed down, the LORD loves the righteous. The LORD watches over the alien and sustains the fatherless and the widow, but he frustrates the ways of the wicked. The LORD reigns forever, your God, O Zion, for all generations. Praise the LORD.

PSALM 146:5–10

 CONNECTION

FAMILY STORIES OF PEACE

Today, connect your family stories to this week's Advent theme of peace. Think about how you can begin sharing your family stories of God's peace.

ENGAGE

Idea 1: Give everyone a piece of paper. Ask each person to write a story or draw a scene when he or she experienced peace. Allow everyone to share his or her thoughts.

Idea 2: Ask everyone in the family to find one possession that helps him or her feel peaceful. Invite each one to share it and to tell why the object is a reminder of peace.

DISCUSS
- What does peace feel like?
- Do you have a story of a family member that experienced God's peace in the midst of a difficult situation?
- How have you spread the peace of God to others?

JOHN THE BAPTIST, PROPHET OF GOD'S PEACE

In our gospel reading today, we focus in on the newborn John. From our readings this week, we know that John is being prepared for faithful service for God's plan. He is born into a family with two upright parents who worship God. We know that God's hand was with him from Gabriel's announcement of his birth. Before John was born, Gabriel declared that the Holy Spirit would be with him, and when Mary visited Elizabeth, this prophecy was fulfilled (v. 41). These events and circumstances clue us in that John is integral to God's plan to bring peace to his people.

Those present following John's birth accordingly raise the question, "What then is this child going to be?" (v. 66). If we follow the story carefully, then Gabriel's announcement has already begun to be fulfilled. So we are compelled to look back to that announcement for our answer. There we learn that John's role is to be one who prepares people for the coming of the Lord (see v. 17).

John's birth is a sign to us that the coming of the Lord is close at hand. John points us to the One who will bring the peace of God. John's character is the embodiment of Advent because he is prepared by God to be a witness who prepares people to receive the Light of the World. Let us embrace John's birth story and recognize our role as a people who cry out, "Prepare the way for the Lord" (3:4).

===== **PRAYER** =====

Hasten the day when in shining light all wrong will stand revealed, when justice will be throned in might, and every hurt be healed; when knowledge, hand in hand with peace, will walk the earth abroad; the day of perfect righteousness, your promised day, O God.[19]

—————— AMEN ——————

FRIDAY ● PEACE THROUGH THE LIGHT

The LORD reigns, he is robed in majesty; the LORD is robed in majesty and is armed with strength. The world is firmly established; it cannot be moved. Your throne was established long ago; you are from all eternity.

— PSALM 93:1–2 —

 CONNECTION

SYMBOLS OF THE SEASON—DOVE

The dove is a symbol of the peace of God. In the Old Testament the dove in the story of Noah was used to discern if the flood waters had gone down and was a sign that God had provided security and land for Noah and his family. The dove continues to be a symbol of comfort and a reminder that God is still present in his creation and working to bring peace through Jesus Christ to the world. As we see the dove this season, let us remember that the first advent announced peace on earth and the second advent will bring that announcement to fulfillment.

ZECHARIAH SINGS OF GOD'S PEACE

At the beginning of Luke we met Zechariah, an upright Jewish priest who was serving in the temple. All of those details were an invitation to respect Zechariah for his place of honor within the Jewish community. Yet when he is visited by a messenger of God, he questions God's plan. This man, who is pictured as godly, lacks faith and loses the ability to speak.

But that is not the end of Zechariah's participation in God's story. Instead, Zechariah becomes for us an example of a person growing in God's grace in preparation for the coming of the Lord. Zechariah reappears in the story when Elizabeth gives birth, and he is asked to name the child. In renewed faith, he obeys God and names the child John. Immediately his mouth opens and we know that God has restored Zechariah as a faithful witness to the coming of the Lord.

Strengthened in faith by God's life-giving action, Zechariah sings about God's plan to bring peace to our world. God is fulfilling the promises that were made to Abraham and his descendants. The One who comes from the house of David is the source of salvation for God's people. John is to become "a prophet of the Most High" and "prepare the way" for the Son of the Most High, who will guide all the people in the way of peace (vv. 76-79).

=== **PRAYER** ===

By the tender mercy of our God, the dawn from on high will break upon us, to give light to those who sit in darkness and in the shadow of death, to guide our feet into the way of peace.

— **LUKE 1:78-79, NRSV** —

SATURDAY • PEACE THROUGH THE LIGHT

Sing to the LORD a new song; sing to the LORD, all the earth. Sing to the LORD, praise his name; proclaim his salvation day after day. Declare his glory among the nations, his marvelous deeds among all peoples.

————— PSALM 96:1–3 —————

 **CONNECTION**

REFLECT ON THE WEEK TOGETHER

- Where did you see God at work in your week?

- What did you learn about peace this week?

- How did you live out God's way of peace?

- Are you ready to celebrate Christmas, the birth of the Son of God?

FAMILY DEVOTIONS
Light the Advent candles • Gospel Reading: Luke 2:1-20

JESUS IS GOD'S PEACE

Jesus is the Savior. He brings the salvation of God. We are invited to remember all the mighty acts of God from ages past. The covenant with Abraham, the Exodus and Sinai epoch, the Promised Land, the Exile and Restoration—all should flood our minds when we think about Jesus bringing God's salvation to his people.

Jesus is the Messiah of Israel. Jesus is the fulfillment of the covenant people's hope in God. In exile God's people cried for One who would be like David. Through the ages the faithful spokesmen of God prophesied about him. Jesus is the desire of the nations. He is the One longed for by an occupied people.

"Jesus is Lord, and Caesar is not" would be the cry of the early church. Jesus is worthy of our whole life. We live for him and him alone.

Jesus is the peace of God for all humanity, with whom God is pleased. He has come to guide us into the healing and restoring way of peace that we were created to live in. God desires that all would come to follow Jesus into the way of peace.

Let's celebrate the Light!

==================== **PRAYER** ====================

Lord Jesus, the Advent candle burns with peace; its radiance calmly glows. The peace the angels foretold we desire entirely. We celebrate your Light.

•————————————— **AMEN** —————————————•

CHRISTMAS SEASON
THE TWELVE DAYS OF CHRISTMAS

FEAST OF THE TABERNACLES
A Devotional Reflection Based on John 1:1-14

"And the Word was made flesh and dwelt [tabernacled] among us" (v. 14, KJV).

Just before dawn, at the mouth of one small limestone cave near Bethlehem, the embers of a small fire are still glowing. Just beyond the opening, a young woman, with her attentive husband at her side, holds a swaddled newborn infant against her breast. From deeper in the cave, she hears the lowing of cattle and the bleating of a goat. But she is captivated by what she sees as she glances out through the cave opening toward the Judean wilderness in the east. There, suspended in the brightening sky, is a double morning star.

"It's beautiful, isn't it, Mary?"

"Yes," she says. She leans her face to the sleeping infant; she hears the short pants, feels the whispers of his breath. The silence of the moment is holy. Just briefly, his eyes flicker open, and Mary sees the Soul of Eternity looking back at her.

"Do you remember what feast begins today?"

"Sukkot. I have not forgotten," she answers. She feels the beating of the divine heart as she hugs him closer.

"We are blessed. God has chosen to tabernacle with us," Joseph says, and lifting his hands, he looks out toward the daystar glowing in the heavens and prays the traditional Sukkot blessing: "Blessed are You, O Lord our God, King of the universe, for keeping us in life, for sustaining us, and for helping us reach this day."[20]

Our Advent journey has brought us at last to Bethlehem on this Christmas Day. Before we enter the stable/cave, we might want to ask, "When was Jesus actually born? What time of the year was it?" The scriptures that illuminate the mysteries of Christmas, that bring us to the manger of divine mercy, may have an answer for us.

Luke gives us one clue. He observes that "shepherds [were] living out in the fields" (Luke 2:8). It is still the custom in the Judean hill country to keep the flocks out on the ranges until bad weather sets in—usually from the middle of March until the middle of October. At twenty-five hundred feet above sea level, Bethlehem can experience cold rains and winds, sometimes even snow flurries, by the middle or end of October. When the weather gets too cold for the flocks, the shepherds bring them in close to town—into stonewalled sheepfolds built in front of the great limestone caves that honeycomb the hills. Because the shepherds were "keeping watch over their flocks at night" (Luke 2:8), we can be fairly certain that the nativity occurred sometime between those months of March and October.

John's gospel provides another, although less obvious, hint that pinpoints the time more precisely. John, of course, does not give a detailed account of the holy nativity as do Matthew and Luke. John's interest is writing the story of the Word who has always existed, the Word who created the cosmos, the Word who gives light to the world. Yet John may be thinking about a particular time when he writes in 1:14 that "the Word became flesh and made his dwelling among us." The King James Version uses the verb "dwelt." The actual intent of the word translated as "dwelt" is "tabernacled." Perhaps John's choice of the word is something we should examine.

In the Old Testament the God of Israel had dwelt in the midst of his people in a holy tent or tabernacle as they wandered in the wilderness. Now he was to be tabernacled among them in a body of flesh. One of the happiest of Jewish feasts is the Feast of Tabernacles, or Sukkot, observed about the first week of October. This joy-filled festival celebrating the autumn harvests in small tabernacles built outside each Jewish home represents the time of restored fellowship with the Lord. Neither Passover nor Pentecost were celebrated with the intensity of joy that Deuteronomy had prescribed for Sukkot: "You shall rejoice in your feast . . . because the LORD your God will bless you in all your produce and in all the work of your hands, so that you will be altogether joyful" (Deut. 16:14-15, RSV). In ancient Israel, the joy of Sukkot was so great that it became known simply as The Feast. It was also known as the Season of Our Joy. During this time, four towering menorahs were lit up, and the priests put on a light show, performing torch dances while the Levites sang and played music. These festivities would occur every night of Sukkot, all through the night.

Now consider Luke's clue, shepherds still out in the fields with their flocks, and John's hint, the Word *tabernacled* among us. Consider the "great joy" of Sukkot, the Feast of Tabernacles, with its images of light and messages of restored fellowship with the Lord, his sheltering care and his provision for our needs. Consider the words of the angel to the shepherds, "Do not be afraid. I bring you good news of great joy that will be for all the people. Today in the town of David a Savior has been born to you; he is Christ the Lord" (Luke 2:10-11). Consider—and rejoice!

We cannot know, nor do we need to know, precisely what time of year Jesus was born, but it does strike us as interesting that Luke and John may be giving us signals—reference points—suggesting to us the Feast of Tabernacles, Sukkot, as the beginning of God's *tabernacling* with us in a body of flesh and blood. Aside from all that, what we do need to know is that "the Word became flesh and made his dwelling among us" (John 1:14).

There he is—the Word is sleeping in the shelter (the tabernacle) of his mother's embrace. *Joy to the world! The Lord is come!*

PREPARE FOR WORSHIP—THE CHRIST CANDLE
Christmas Day

The fifth candle in the Advent wreath is the Christ candle. Christ, God's chosen one, is the long-awaited hope that was announced by the prophets and is yearned for today. He is the beacon of love that shines from the little town of Bethlehem and that we desire to see in the New Jerusalem. He is the reason meek shepherds once rejoiced in the fields and his wounded church will celebrate on the day of the Lord. He is God's message of peace to an occupied Jewish people two thousand years ago, and he is the heart's cry for peace today. Jesus Christ, Immanuel, God with us in the flesh, is all the reason we will ever need to celebrate! Let us celebrate with all we have, because our God has come and our God will come again.

Praise God, from whom all blessings flow;
Praise Him, all creatures here below;
Praise Him above, you heavenly host;
Praise Father, Son, and Holy Ghost.[21]

— AMEN —

SECOND DAY OF CHRISTMAS
Light the Christ candle

The one who comes from above is above all; the one who is from the earth belongs to the earth, and speaks as one from the earth. The one who comes from heaven is above all. He testifies to what he has seen and heard, but no one accepts his testimony. The man who has accepted it has certified that God is truthful. For the one whom God has sent speaks the words of God, for God gives the Spirit without limit. The Father loves the Son and has placed everything in his hands. Whoever believes in the Son has eternal life, but whoever rejects the Son will not see life, for God's wrath remains on him.

— JOHN 3:31–36 —

CELEBRATE THE LIGHT

Praise God for all his glory. Try to think of as many characteristics of God that convey his power and glory as you can. Take the list and create a family prayer.

THIRD DAY OF CHRISTMAS

Light the Christ candle

Sing to the LORD a new song;
sing to the LORD, all the earth.
Sing to the LORD, praise his name;
proclaim his salvation day after day.
Declare his glory among the nations,
his marvelous deeds among all peoples.
For great is the LORD and most worthy of praise;
he is to be feared above all gods.
For all the gods of the nations are idols,
but the LORD made the heavens.
Splendor and majesty are before him;
strength and glory are in his sanctuary.
Ascribe to the LORD, O families of nations,
ascribe to the LORD glory and strength.
Ascribe to the LORD the glory due his name;
bring an offering and come into his courts.
Worship the LORD in the splendor of his holiness;
tremble before him, all the earth.

———————— **PSALM 96:1–9** ————————

CELEBRATE THE LIGHT

Sing your favorite Christmas carols. Have everyone in the family
pick one to sing.

FOURTH DAY OF CHRISTMAS
Light the Christ candle

He is the image of the invisible God, the firstborn over all creation. For by him all things were created: things in heaven and on earth, visible and invisible, whether thrones or powers or rulers or authorities; all things were created by him and for him. He is before all things, and in him all things hold together. And he is the head of the body, the church; he is the beginning and the firstborn from among the dead, so that in everything he might have the supremacy. For God was pleased to have all his fullness dwell in him, and through him to reconcile to himself all things, whether things on earth or things in heaven, by making peace through his blood, shed on the cross.

COL. 1:15–20

CELEBRATE THE LIGHT

Share with one another how God has shown his strength to you in providing, protecting, or forgiving.

FIFTH DAY OF CHRISTMAS

Light the Christ candle

The elder,

To the chosen lady and her children, whom I love in the truth—and not I only, but also all who know the truth—because of the truth, which lives in us and will be with us forever:

Grace, mercy and peace from God the Father and from Jesus Christ, the Father's Son, will be with us in truth and love.

It has given me great joy to find some of your children walking in the truth, just as the Father commanded us. And now, dear lady, I am not writing you a new command but one we have had from the beginning. I ask that we love one another. And this is love: that we walk in obedience to his commands. As you have heard from the beginning, his command is that you walk in love.

 2 JOHN 1-6

CELEBRATE THE LIGHT

Come up with a random act of kindness you can do for someone this week. Spread the good news of Christmas by spreading the love of Jesus to others.

SIXTH DAY OF CHRISTMAS
Light the Christ candle

In bringing many sons to glory, it was fitting that God, for whom and through whom everything exists, should make the author of their salvation perfect through suffering. Both the one who makes men holy and those who are made holy are of the same family. So Jesus is not ashamed to call them brothers. He says, "I will declare your name to my brothers; in the presence of the congregation I will sing your praises."

And again, "I will put my trust in him."

And again he says, "Here am I, and the children God has given me."

Since the children have flesh and blood, he too shared in their humanity so that by his death he might destroy him who holds the power of death—that is, the devil—and free those who all their lives were held in slavery by their fear of death. For surely it is not angels he helps, but Abraham's descendants. For this reason he had to be made like his brothers in every way, in order that he might become a merciful and faithful high priest in service to God, and that he might make atonement for the sins of the people. Because he himself suffered when he was tempted, he is able to help those who are being tempted.

—————————— HEB. 2:10–18 ——————————

CELEBRATE THE LIGHT

It's amazing that the Son of God was born as a human and calls us brothers and sisters. Talk with one another about what it means to be a child of God.

SEVENTH DAY OF CHRISTMAS

Light the Christ candle

Some time later, Jesus went up to Jerusalem for a feast of the Jews. Now there is in Jerusalem near the Sheep Gate a pool, which in Aramaic is called Bethesda and which is surrounded by five covered colonnades. Here a great number of disabled people used to lie—the blind, the lame, the paralyzed. One who was there had been an invalid for thirty-eight years. When Jesus saw him lying there and learned that he had been in this condition for a long time, he asked him, "Do you want to get well?"

"Sir," the invalid replied, "I have no one to help me into the pool when the water is stirred. While I am trying to get in, someone else goes down ahead of me."

Then Jesus said to him, "Get up! Pick up your mat and walk." At once the man was cured; he picked up his mat and walked.

The day on which this took place was a Sabbath, and so the Jews said to the man who had been healed, "It is the Sabbath; the law forbids you to carry your mat."

But he replied, "The man who made me well said to me, 'Pick up your mat and walk.'"

So they asked him, "Who is this fellow who told you to pick it up and walk?"

The man who was healed had no idea who it was, for Jesus had slipped away into the crowd that was there.

Later Jesus found him at the temple and said to him, "See, you are well again. Stop sinning or something worse may happen to you." The man went away and told the Jews that it was Jesus who had made him well.

—— JOHN 5:1–15 ——

CELEBRATE THE LIGHT

Pray for those in your church family who are sick. Talk about how you can encourage them this week.

EIGHTH DAY OF CHRISTMAS
Light the Christ candle

When the time of their purification according to the Law of Moses had been completed, Joseph and Mary took him to Jerusalem to present him to the Lord (as it is written in the Law of the Lord, "Every firstborn male is to be consecrated to the Lord"), and to offer a sacrifice in keeping with what is said in the Law of the Lord: "a pair of doves or two young pigeons."

Now there was a man in Jerusalem called Simeon, who was righteous and devout. He was waiting for the consolation of Israel, and the Holy Spirit was upon him. It had been revealed to him by the Holy Spirit that he would not die before he had seen the Lord's Christ. Moved by the Spirit, he went into the temple courts. When the parents brought in the child Jesus to do for him what the custom of the Law required, Simeon took him in his arms and praised God, saying:

> "Sovereign Lord, as you have promised,
> you now dismiss your servant in peace.
> For my eyes have seen your salvation,
> which you have prepared in the sight of all people,
> a light for revelation to the Gentiles
> and for glory to your people Israel."

The child's father and mother marveled at what was said about him. Then Simeon blessed them and said to Mary, his mother: "This child is destined to cause the falling and rising of many in Israel, and to be a sign that will be spoken against, so that the thoughts of many hearts will be revealed. And a sword will pierce your own soul too."

There was also a prophetess, Anna, the daughter of Phanuel, of the tribe of Asher. She was very old; she had lived with her husband seven years after her marriage, and then was a widow until she was eighty-four. She never left the temple but worshiped night and day, fasting and praying. Coming up to them at that very moment, she gave thanks to God and spoke about the child to all who were looking forward to the redemption of Jerusalem.

When Joseph and Mary had done everything required by the Law of the Lord, they returned to Galilee to their own town of Nazareth. And the child grew and became strong; he was filled with wisdom, and the grace of God was upon him.

LUKE 2:22-40

CELEBRATE THE LIGHT

Jesus is the fulfillment of God's promise to bless and restore Israel. Share with one another the hopes you have for your future and any promises God has made you.

NINTH DAY OF CHRISTMAS
Light the Christ candle

At this the Jews began to grumble about him because he said, "I am the bread that came down from heaven." They said, "Is this not Jesus, the son of Joseph, whose father and mother we know? How can he now say, 'I came down from heaven'?"

"Stop grumbling among yourselves," Jesus answered. "No one can come to me unless the Father who sent me draws him, and I will raise him up at the last day. It is written in the Prophets: 'They will all be taught by God.' Everyone who listens to the Father and learns from him comes to me. No one has seen the Father except the one who is from God; only he has seen the Father. I tell you the truth, he who believes has everlasting life."

— JOHN 6:41–47 —

CELEBRATE THE LIGHT

Share with one another what you have been learning from God today.

TENTH DAY OF CHRISTMAS

Light the Christ candle

When evening came, his disciples went down to the lake, where they got into a boat and set off across the lake for Capernaum. By now it was dark, and Jesus had not yet joined them. A strong wind was blowing and the waters grew rough. When they had rowed three or three and a half miles, they saw Jesus approaching the boat, walking on the water; and they were terrified. But he said to them, "It is I; don't be afraid." Then they were willing to take him into the boat, and immediately the boat reached the shore where they were heading.

The next day the crowd that had stayed on the opposite shore of the lake realized that only one boat had been there, and that Jesus had not entered it with his disciples, but that they had gone away alone. Then some boats from Tiberias landed near the place where the people had eaten the bread after the Lord had given thanks. Once the crowd realized that neither Jesus nor his disciples were there, they got into the boats and went to Capernaum in search of Jesus.

— JOHN 6:16–24 —

CELEBRATE THE LIGHT

Rest today knowing that the child in the manger is both Lord of creation and our Savior.

ELEVENTH DAY OF CHRISTMAS
Light the Christ candle

As he went along, he saw a man blind from birth. His disciples asked him, "Rabbi, who sinned, this man or his parents, that he was born blind?"

"Neither this man nor his parents sinned," said Jesus, "but this happened so that the work of God might be displayed in his life. As long as it is day, we must do the work of him who sent me. Night is coming, when no one can work. While I am in the world, I am the light of the world."

Having said this, he spit on the ground, made some mud with the saliva, and put it on the man's eyes. "Go," he told him, "wash in the Pool of Siloam" (this word means Sent). So the man went and washed, and came home seeing.

His neighbors and those who had formerly seen him begging asked, "Isn't this the same man who used to sit and beg?" Some claimed that he was.

Others said, "No, he only looks like him."

But he himself insisted, "I am the man."

"How then were your eyes opened?" they demanded.

He replied, "The man they call Jesus made some mud and put it on my eyes. He told me to go to Siloam and wash. So I went and washed, and then I could see."

"Where is this man?" they asked him.

"I don't know," he said.

———————————— JOHN 9:1–12 ————————————

CELEBRATE THE LIGHT
"By the tender mercy of our God, the dawn from on high will break upon us, to give light to those who sit in darkness and in the shadow of death, to guide our feet into the way of peace" (Luke 1:78-79, NRSV).

Praise God for Jesus fulfilling what was written about him.

TWELFTH DAY OF CHRISTMAS

Light the Christ candle

On his arrival, Jesus found that Lazarus had already been in the tomb for four days. Bethany was less than two miles from Jerusalem, and many Jews had come to Martha and Mary to comfort them in the loss of their brother. When Martha heard that Jesus was coming, she went out to meet him, but Mary stayed at home.

"Lord," Martha said to Jesus, "if you had been here, my brother would not have died. But I know that even now God will give you whatever you ask."

Jesus said to her, "Your brother will rise again."

Martha answered, "I know he will rise again in the resurrection at the last day."

Jesus said to her, "I am the resurrection and the life. He who believes in me will live, even though he dies; and whoever lives and believes in me will never die. Do you believe this?"

"Yes, Lord," she told him, "I believe that you are the Christ, the Son of God, who was to come into the world."

———————— JOHN 11:17-27 ————————

CELEBRATE THE LIGHT

He is the Christ, the Son of God, who has come into the world. Write or draw your favorite memory from the Advent and Christmas season and share it with one another.

NOTES

1. Adapted from Reginald Heber, "Hosanna to the Living Lord" (1811), Cyber Hymnal, http://www.hymntime.com/tch/htm/h/t/htliving.htm.

2. Adapted from John M. Neale, "O Very God of Very God" (1846), Cyber Hymnal, http://www.hymntime.com/tch/htm/o/v/overygod.htm.

3. Adapted from "The King Shall Come When Morning Dawns" (1907), author unknown, trans. John Brownlie, Cyber Hymnal, http://www.hymntime.com/tch/htm/k/i/kingcome.htm.

4. Adapted from Phillip P. Hiller, "O Son of God, We Wait for Thee," trans. Joseph A. Seiss (1890), Cyber Hymnal, http://www.hymntime.com/tch/htm/o/s/o/osonogod.htm.

5. Adapted from Johann Heerman, "O Christ, Our True and Only Light" (1630), trans. Catherine Winkworth (1858), Cyber Hymnal, http://www.hymntime.com/tch/htm/o/c/ocotruea.htm.

6. Adapted from Douglas L. Rights, "Veiled in Darkness Judah Lay" (1915), Cyber Hymnal, http://www.hymntime.com/tch/htm/v/e/i/veildark.htm.

7. Adapted from George Weissel, "Lift Up Your Heads, Ye Mighty Gates" (1642), trans. Catherine Winkworth (1855), Cyber Hymnal, http://www.hymntime.com/tch/htm/l/u/lupyhymg.htm.

8. Adapted from Valentin Thilo, "Ye Sons of Men, Oh, Hearken" (1642), trans. Arthur T. Russell (1851), Cyber Hymnal, http://www.hymntime.com/tch/htm/y/s/ysmheark.htm.

9. Adapted from Charles Wesley, "Come, Thou Long Expected Jesus" (1745), Cyber Hymnal, http://www.hymntime.com/tch/htm/c/o/m/comtlong.htm.

10. Adapted from Judson W. Van DeVenter, "I Wandered in the Shades of Night" (1897), Cyber Hymnal, http://www.cyberhymnal.org/htm/i/w/iwanderd.htm.

11. Adapted from Thomas T. Lynch, "Lift Up Your Heads, Rejoice" (1856), Cyber Hymnal, http://www.cyberhymnal.org/htm/l/u/lupyhrej.htm.

12. Adapted from Charles Wesley, "Christ, Whose Glory Fills the Skies" (1740), Cyber Hymnal, http://www.cyberhymnal.org/htm/c/w/cwgfthes.htm.

13. Adapted from "Hark! A Thrilling Voice Is Sounding" (5th c.), author unknown, trans. Edward Caswall (1849), Cyber Hymnal, http://www.cyberhymnal.org/htm/h/t/hthrillv.htm.

14. Adapted from Luther B. Bridgers, "He Keeps Me Singing" (1910), Cyber Hymnal, http://www.cyberhymnal.org/htm/h/k/hkeepsme.htm.

15. Adapted from "The Lord Is Coming" (ca. 1849), author unknown, Cyber Hymnal, http://hymntime.com/tch/htm/l/o/r/lordisco.htm.

16. Adapted from Johan O. Wallin, "Jerusalem, Lift Up Thy Voice" (1814), trans. Ernst W. Olsen, Cyber Hymnal, http://www.cyberhymnal.org/htm/j/l/jliftutv.htm.

17. Adapted from Charles Wesley, "Light of Those Whose Dreary Dwelling" (1745), Cyber Hymnal, http://www.cyberhymnal.org/htm/l/i/litofwdd.htm.

18. Adapted from Bernard of Morlaix, "The World Is Very Evil" (12th c.), trans. John M. Neale (1858), Cyber Hymnal, http://www.cyberhymnal.org/htm/w/o/worldisv.htm.

19. Adapted from Frederick L. Hosmer, "Thy Kingdom Come, on Bended Knee" (1891), Cyber Hymnal, http://www.cyberhymnal.org/htm/t/h/thykcobk.htm.

20. Robin Sampson, "The Biblical Holy Day of Sukkot," Congregation Netzar Torah Yeshua, http://messianicfellowship.50webs.com/wisdomsukkot.html# (accessed May 9, 2011).

21. Adapted from Thomsas Ken, "Praise God, from Whom All Blessings Flow" (1674), Cyber Hymnal, http://www.cyberhymnal.org/htm/p/r/praisegf.htm.

BIBLIOGRAPHY

Beasley-Topliffe, Keith, ed. *Loving God Through the Darkness: Selected Writings of John of the Cross.* Nashville: Upper Room Books, 2000.

Bratcher, Dennis. "The Season of Advent: Anticipation and Hope." CRI/Voice Institute. http://crivoice.org/cyadvent.html (accessed April 3, 2010).

Craddock, Fred B. *Luke.* Interpretation: A Bible Commentary for Teaching and Preaching. Louisville, Ky.: John Knox Press, 1990.

Green, Joel B. *The Gospel of Luke.* New International Commentary on the New Testament. Grand Rapids: William B. Eerdmans, 1997.

Hahn, Roger L. *Matthew: A Commentary for Bible Students.* Wesleyan Bible Commentary Series. Indianapolis: Wesleyan Publishing House, 2007.

Hare, Douglas R. *Matthew.* Interpretation: A Bible Commentary for Teaching and Preaching. Louisville, Ky.: John Knox Press, 1993.

Harper, Steve. *Devotional Life in the Wesleyan Tradition.* Nashville: Upper Room, 1983.

Job, Rueben P. *A Wesleyan Spiritual Reader.* Nashville: Abingdon Press, 1998.

Job, Rueben P., and Norman Shawchuck. *A Guide to Prayer for Ministers and Other Servants.* Nashville: Upper Room, 1983.

Peterson, Eugene H. *A Long Obedience in the Same Direction: Discipleship in an Instant Society.* Downers Grove, Ill.: InterVarsity Press, 1980.

Steffler, Alva William. *Symbols of the Christian Faith.* Grand Rapids: William B. Eerdmans, 2002.

Waller, Gary Lee. *Celebrations and Observances of the Church Year: Leading Meaningful Services from Advent to All Saints' Day.* Kansas City: Beacon Hill Press of Kansas City, 2009.

Witvliet, John D., and David Vroege, eds. *Proclaiming the Christmas Gospel: Ancient Sermons and Hymns for Contemporary Christian Inspiration.* Grand Rapids: Baker Books, 2004.

Yaconelli, Mark. *Wonder, Fear, and Longing: A Book of Prayers.* Grand Rapids: Zondervan, 2009.